Learning to Read, Step by Step!

Ready to Read   Preschool–Kindergarten
• big type and easy words • rhyme and rhythm • picture clues
For children who know the alphabet and are eager to
begin reading.

Reading with Help   Preschool–Grade 1
• basic vocabulary • short sentences • simple stories
For children who recognize familiar words and sound out
new words with help.

Reading on Your Own   Grades 1–3
• engaging characters • easy-to-follow plots • popular topics
For children who are ready to read on their own.

Reading Paragraphs   Grades 2–3
• challenging vocabulary • short paragraphs • exciting stories
For newly independent readers who read simple sentences
with confidence.

Ready for Chapters   Grades 2–4
• chapters • longer paragraphs • full-color art
For children who want to take the plunge into chapter books
but still like colorful pictures.

STEP INTO READING® is designed to give every child a successful
reading experience. The grade levels are only guides; children will progress
through the steps at their own speed, developing confidence in their reading.
The F&P Text Level on the back cover serves as another tool to help you
choose the right book for your child.

Remember, a lifetime love of reading starts with a single step!

*In memory of my great-great-great-grandmother,
Minerva Bell Lewis, born enslaved in 1844.
Once emancipated, she would become the first
Black female property owner in her hometown of
Scottsville, Virginia. She and her husband, G. W. Lewis,
also formerly enslaved, had thirteen children,
five of whom became teachers.
—S.D.W.*

*In memory of my grandparents for their unconditional
love, support, and perseverance
—K.H.*

Text copyright © 2022 by Sharon Dennis Wyeth
Cover art and interior illustrations copyright © 2022 by Kim Holt

All rights reserved. Published in the United States by Random House Children's Books, a division of Penguin Random House LLC, New York.

Step into Reading, Random House, and the Random House colophon are registered trademarks of Penguin Random House LLC.

Visit us on the Web!
StepIntoReading.com
rhcbooks.com

Educators and librarians, for a variety of teaching tools, visit us at RHTeachersLibrarians.com

Library of Congress Cataloging-in-Publication Data is available upon request.
ISBN 978-0-593-43478-9 (trade) — ISBN 978-0-593-43479-6 (lib. bdg.) —
ISBN 978-0-593-43480-2 (ebook)

Printed in the United States of America
10 9 8 7 6 5 4 3 2
First Edition

This book has been officially leveled by using the F&P Text Level Gradient™ Leveling System.

JUNETEENTH
Our Day of Freedom

by Sharon Dennis Wyeth
illustrated by Kim Holt

Random House 🏠 New York

Juneteenth is a joyous holiday!
It is also called Freedom Day.
On that day, we celebrate
the end of slavery in America.

Juneteenth got its name
from June 19.

On that date in 1865,
Major General Gordon Granger
entered the city of
Galveston, Texas.
About two thousand Union
soldiers were with him.

Some of the soldiers belonged to the United States Colored Troops, also known as the USCT.

The USCT soldiers were free
African Americans.
Some had made dangerous escapes
from where they had been
enslaved.

They had joined the Union Army
to fight for the freedom of
their own people.

From April 1861 to April 1865,
America had been at war
over slavery.
It was called the Civil War.

Eleven states that allowed slavery
had rebelled and left the Union.
Texas was one of them.
But the rebel states had lost.

Even before the war ended,
President Lincoln had signed
the order called
the Emancipation Proclamation.

On January 1, 1863,
he declared that
all enslaved people
in the rebel states
were to be freed.

Yet two years later, in 1865, thousands of African Americans in Texas still hadn't been told they were free!

Enslaved people did
backbreaking work for no pay.
Slaveholders had selfishly kept
the good news of freedom
a secret.
They did not want to lose
their unpaid workers.

But now General Granger
had come to read Order No. 3,
to proclaim freedom.
The soldiers would make sure
the order was obeyed.

Granger's voice rang out!

"All slaves are free. . . ."

The crowd grew excited.

Enslaved people shouted for joy.

When they discovered that
they could have been freed
two years earlier,
many were stunned
and angry, too.

Some enslaved people had tried
to run away in the past.
But if caught,
they were harshly punished.

As the good news spread,
enslaved laborers walked
out of the fields.
They could no longer be
forced to plant and harvest crops
for no pay.

Enslaved servants left the
large houses where slaveholders had
forced them to cook,
wash clothes,
and take care of farm animals.
Now, at last, they were free!

Imagine how thankful they felt!
They knelt in prayer.

Imagine their gladness and
celebrations!

Neighbors hugged
and shared the good things
they had!

There might have been
sweet strawberry drinks,
corn bread with apple butter,
or a pot of delicious stew.

Thousands left their
tiny slave cabins behind.
Freedom meant they could
set out to make new lives.
They had few belongings.

But they had powerful dreams.

Dreams they could share

as they walked.

Dreams they could share

around campfires of Union soldiers

who took them in.

The newly freed people wanted
their own land.

They dreamed of building houses
and starting farms.

Slaveholders had tried to prevent
enslaved people from
learning to read and write.
Now newly freed people had a
chance to learn.
They were eager for an education.

Most of all, they wanted
to work for wages!
They took their skills with them
wherever they went.

Field hands and cowhands,
carpenters and blacksmiths,
seamstresses and cooks
could now be paid for their labors.

Not all freed people in Texas
left the state.
Some became tenant farmers and
servants for former slaveholders.

This was a hard life, too.

The wages were low,

but people were paid.

Freed people often
gave themselves new names
for their new lives!
Names of lost loved ones or
the places where they were born.
Names from the Bible or a poem.
African names passed down
in secret.

People named themselves
for the things they believed in—
Truth and Freedom.

Freedom made them hopeful!

But they would not easily forget
the cruelty of slavery.

Many families had been separated
and never saw one another again.

June 19 became a
day of remembrance
in Texas.
It is a day when
the descendants of
enslaved African Americans
think about their ancestors.

And, like those
who came before them,
they celebrate freedom.

In 1980, Texas made
Juneteenth a state holiday.
Juneteenth became celebrated
in nearly every other state and
the District of Columbia.

In 2021,
Juneteenth was made a
federal holiday.
People line the streets at
Juneteenth parades
to see brightly decorated floats
and marching bands.

In Longview, Texas,
there's a Juneteenth rodeo!

On Juneteenth,
we play baseball!

We have Juneteenth block parties.
Everyone on the street is invited.

We bring homemade salads and
desserts to backyard barbecues.

We enjoy red foods:
watermelon, red velvet cake,
and strawberry soda,
a traditional Juneteenth drink.

Our elders tell the stories of
our ancestors' lives.
We pass around family photos
and draw family trees.

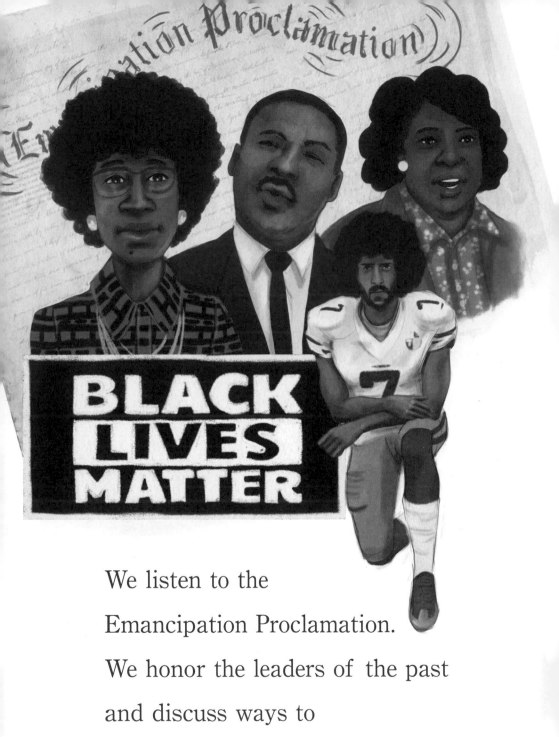

We listen to the

Emancipation Proclamation.

We honor the leaders of the past

and discuss ways to

keep working for equality.

We sing the

Black National Anthem.

"Lift every voice and sing. . . ."

We write essays

about what freedom means to us.

America was founded

on the promise of freedom

in the Declaration of

Independence,

signed in 1776.

With the end of slavery in 1865,

the country got one step closer

to keeping that promise.

Juneteenth is a celebration of

freedom for all!

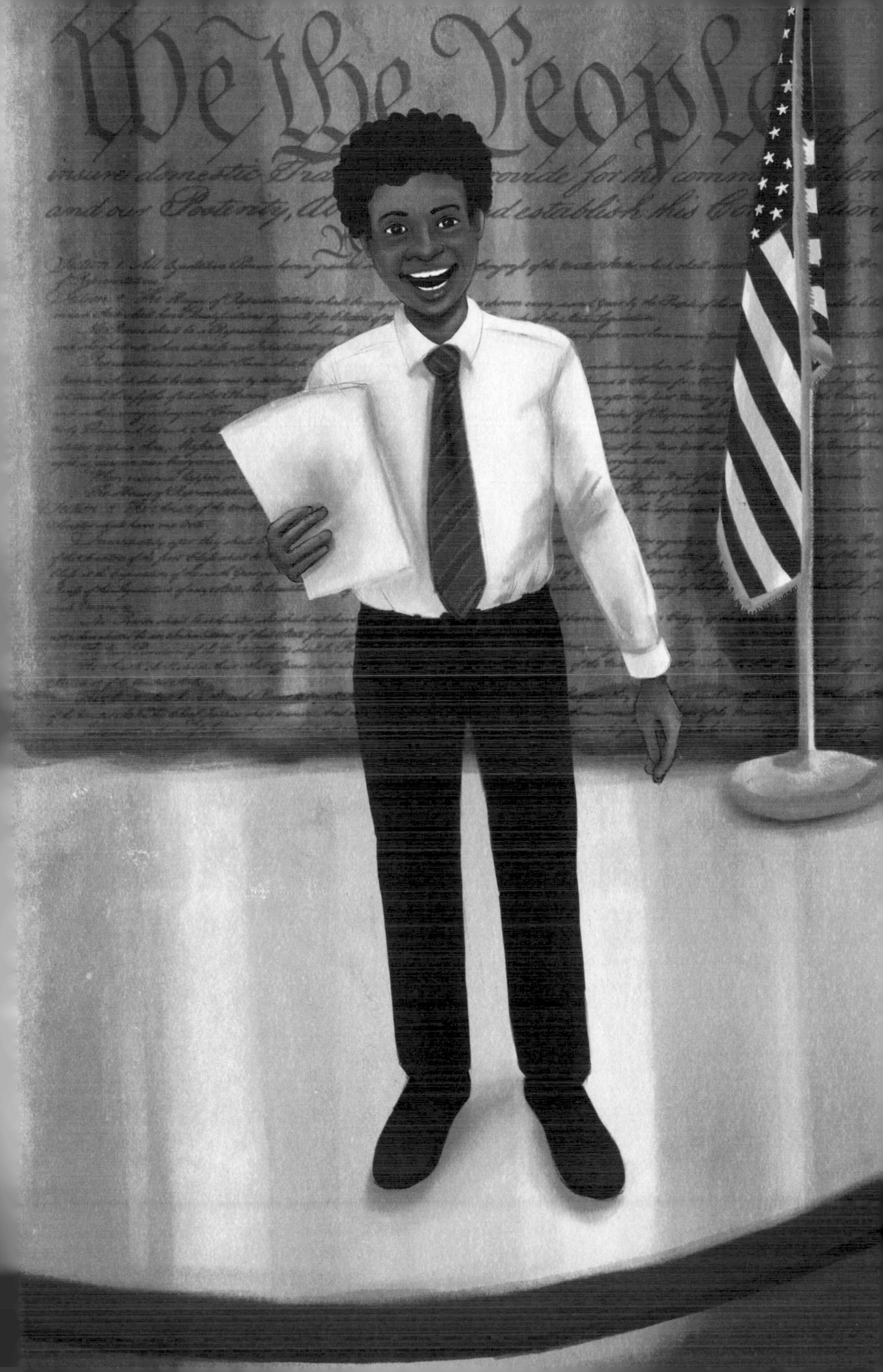
We the Peopl

Author's Note

The long-denied freedom of 250,000 enslaved people in Texas has become a powerful symbol. But slavery was not abolished in the entire country until the Thirteenth Amendment was ratified on December 6, 1865. Through political activism and participation in the democratic process, our country continues to strive to meet the high ideals of its Declaration of Independence and Constitution.